Introduction

Understanding the tough notion of "Respect" is an essential virtue that everyone should strive to uphold in their society.

We might have trouble finding the exact words to explain what you want to say about respect, however, when grasped, it has the power to permanently change a person's life.

In this part of the series we'll learn the following:
*What's respect.
*Strategies to be respected.
*Showing differences and reciprocity.
*Identifying potential solutions.

*Concluding remarks.

Throughout the "Respect a key tool to living a successful life series, you'll discover all this stated above and more.

We must decide what kind of meal we want to make before we can begin to prepare it. To make macaroni and cheese, for example we wouldn't use a recipe for chicken soup. The life journey is no different. Should someone be successful, one must first adopt the idea that success is what they want, and respect is one of the tools they need to find before they can locate success.

What's respect

Though it can take many forms, respect is fundamentally the act of treating someone with worth, dignity and regard. It entails being kind and nice to others and respecting their viewpoints. Respect for one another is the foundation for healthy and improved relationships in our groups, which in turn fosters peace in our schools, businesses,, countries, and global community.

The most prevalent of the many important ramifications that come with respect are as follows:

Makes everything just and fair for

everyone.
Enhances and encourages
constructive interactions.

Encourages knowledge exchanges
without bias.
Gives one a sensation and impression
of security.
Enhances general well-being and
trust encourages interpersonal and
group development, and
socialization.
Makes one feel satisfied with life.

You'll probably receive whatever you
want with a modicum of respect
after you are on good terms with
every member of your society. On

the other hand, you'll struggle since you won't receive the respect you deserve. Respecting other people may not mean anything to you, but it may mean everything to them. Therefore, why won't I do it if there is anything I can do to have a nice life and be content at all times in a positive frame of mind?

I speak to everyone in the same way, whether he is the garbage man or the president of the university.Albert Einstein.

I asked a few of my friends what respect is and their ideas really got me thinking.

Even if you can not change all the people around you, you can change the people you choose to be around. Life is too short to waste your time on people who don't respect, appreciate, and value you. Spend your life with people who make you smile, laugh, and feel loved. Roy. T. Bennett.

Respect is a reciprocal giving to a person or someone that has the right that can be qualified to. Esther.

In this definition respect is described as having a qualification to the right. In light of Esther's

Concept, I ought to respect people who deserve it based on how they've reciprocally shown it to me.

In another's definition she said " well to me without a dictionary" it is reverence and honor given to someone whether old or young. Jedidah.

Jedidah defines respect as something that people ought to have for one another, regardless of their age, social station, worth, or ethnicity. Everyone who deserve it should see it.

Note: Respect is not a privilege.

Thus, instead of forcing respect, learn to earn it.

Food for thought: Should I respect people exclusively in return for their respect?
In what ways have I previously disrespected others?
In the past how did I force respect?
And how might I earn it now?

Ways to gain respect.

In many different ways, people have gained respect throughout history, from the BC to the AD. Respect has always been highly prized and is a factor in people's contentment.

When you earn someone's respect, you are accorded more respect in return for your deeds that prove you deserve it.
The foundation of every human interaction is Respect.

We all want to be treated with respect and gratitude, regardless of our age or financial situation.
Treating others with respect demonstrates their value and worth

Respect is essential in any kind of interaction.

Make improvements, not excuses. seek respect, not attention. Roy T. Bennett.

These are the primary ways that people gain respect.
* Achievements
* Bribes
* Fear of punishment
* Culture
* Conscience.

To gain a basic understanding of these techniques, we'll go over each one individually.

Through achievements:

Everybody has mentors in their lives. These individuals have earned recognition for the things they did differently to change our society and have either positively or negatively impacted our lives. A person's accomplishments have an impact on how many others dress, speak, act, or even go about their daily lives. Does this have to be the case.

"There are lot of people I admire and respect, but I don't necessarily want to be like them. I am too happy being myself". James D'arcy.

When a person wears a wrong combination of dress, almost everyone they come in contact with will comment on how awful the dress code looks. If, however a well known artist releases an album and appears in one of his videos wearing the same outfit, within weeks the outfit will become the talk of the town. We've seen people exhibit little regard for their thoughts, bodies, or even beliefs simply because someone has achieved their state of mind or way of life.

If all I do is based on what others do, I haven't begun to live because I do nothing. There's nothing wrong with having a mentor but it is incorrect to appreciate someone just for something they have done what if they haven't?

Through Bribe:

The first thing that springs to mind when we hear the word "bribe" is money, but bribes go beyond that. Some years ago, in the neighborhood where I resided, a political party was running a campaign for their candidate for a government seat.

 Most political parties are well-known for getting people to vote for their candidates, but this was not the case with this party.
What piqued my interest was a group of women I met on the way who grumbled and said if they don't give us this certain amountwe won't vote

vote for their party.

"Bribery is the offering, giving, receiving, or soliciting of any item of value in order to influence the action of an official or other person in charge of a public or legal duty," according to Wikipedia.

The women in my narrative didn't care about what the political party or its candidate had done for the country; all they cared about was money. Dissregarding their country's laws.

According to a study conducted in Papua New Guinea, cultural norms are the main cause of corruption. Bribery is a common method of

Obtaining public services in Papua New Guinea. Rather than being unlawful conduct, bribery is viewed as a means of generating "quick money and sustaining life."

Furthermore, when corruption becomes a cultural norm, criminal acts such as bribery are no longer seen as terrible, the clear borders that once separated between legal and illegal acts are lost, and judgments are based on opinion rather than a code of conduct. Where there is no law, there is no offense.

Which brings us to our next topic. Culture.

Through Culture :

The cultures that govern any group or society are what distinguishes them.

Everybody's life is heavily influenced by culture, as it doesn't require comprehension for it to do so. In the past, most of Africa accepted human sacrifice as a common practice. With a great number of innocent people losing their lives due to this ideology.

This culture was revered since it had been there for a very long time. As a result, many people believed that it was something that had to be done

Or else a "Higher being" would punish the society, and this mentality was been passed down through the centuries. Additionally, anyone who defies this traditional concept faces death or other harsh consequences, which instills terror.

There's a Yoruba proverb that says. The fact that you greet doesn't imply that you have good manners.

That I obey a rule or adhere to a belief does not mean I respect it; respect is based on the human being not on a cultural ideology.

Should you be respected if you

damage the person you see because of a belief you can't see?

Fear of retribution :

Many people know what is right but do nothing because they are afraid of being penalized or labeled cowards.
Fear as long been a major impediment to respect.

Because they're afraid what may happen to them, many people have respected more or less than they should. I recall being invited to teach some students once on how to play drums. During our meetings I found that one learned quickly, and put everything into practice in matter of minutes.

While not even the other was picking up. I kept asking, "what was the problem?" and most of the time I felt upset. However, I later found out he was not even ready to try; it would have been acceptable if he had made some few mistakes, but his fear had taken a greater part of him and prevented him from learning.
I didn't intend to punish him. But he has low self-esteem as a result of his past experiences with instructors and maybe his parents.

Like this child, most people do not speak up when they think something is wrong giving the government, and their superiors respect because they fear to be punished, even when the government or superior are wrong.

Most people like this youngster, don't feel they'll ever get it right because others have talked them down or even punished them; they look down on themselves and have this I can't do it mindset.

When we treat people merely as they are, they will remain as they are. When we them as if they were what they should be, they will become what they should be. " - Thomas S. Monson.

Its our responsibility to make our

surroundings a safe sanctuary for those who require it. Teach people to respect rather than to fear.

Through force:

Force can be said as the coercion or compulsion, especially with the use of threat or violence.
Making people go against their will.
Google.

Force is doing things against your will because there's an higher power compulsing you to do it. Force almost like fear but isn't fear.

The slave trade Era is a good example of getting respect through force. The slaves had no choice but to obey their slave masters against their will because there's a higher power compulsing them.

Most criminals in prison are not happy about being in the prison but there's an higher power the law which wouldn't let them go.

Good news is force isn't really a bad way to get respect REALLY!!? Yeah it isn't, if it doesn't compromises on your self respect it isn't a wrong thing.
If I'm forced to what will bring out the best in me is it wrong?

We all have that moment we were forced and we weren't happy about it but later in the future we'll see why that action was taken either by our parents, friends or relations and we show the person who forced us to taking that action more respect, because by that action we also have gained more respect.

There once, was a king who struggled to find a spouse for his daughter, since she was the most beautiful of all. He decided that the person who will marry her must be brave, so he invited all the young men in the village who are interested in marrying the princess to a contest.

He then led them all to the bank of

most dreadful river in the land and declared that whoever swims across will marry the princess.

Most of the men instantly went back and gave up, but one brave jumped jumped in and was devoured immediately by crocodiles.

A young man who hadn't given up hope of seeing this turned around to leave, but his friend stopped him, he disagreed but his friend still insisted after so many arguments he decided to stay, on getting to the river bank and seeing the crocodiles eating what was remaining of the who had gone in thought to go back he was just thinking about it when his friend pushed him in.

He fell in the river and made a loud crash sound the crocodiles on hearing this swam to hide themselves feeling there was danger.

He started swimming as fast as he could the crocodiles on discovering it was a human chased after him,he swam even faster and got to the other end before the crocodiles could get to him.

The king and everyone watching clapped and were amazed about what has happened. And he was married to the princess.

One thing that baffles me whenever I think of this story is who did the work, the young man, or his friend?

If this had 20th century, he would have hosted a swimming class where even the king would go to learn how to swim in a river filled with crocodiles, his success would happen rapidly.

Thats why first you must think of the end result, and be ready to stand on your decision either it be yes or no.

Note: You are the best person that knows what is right for don't be fooled. Learn to think with understanding.

You actually can't force people to respect you, respect is something that comes as a result of your values and the way you act on them. So the people we are to obey when forced are people with values, people with results.

Through the conscience :

Conscience can be defined as a person's moral sense of right and wrong, acting as a guide to one's behavior.

I once picked up a woman from a garbage dump as she was burning with fever; she was in her last days and her only lament was: "my son did this to me".

I begged her: you must forgive your son. In a moment of madness, when he wasn't himself, he did a thing he regrets. Be a mother for him, forgive him. It took me a long time to her say. " I forgive my son*. Just before she died in my arms, she was able to say that with a real forgiveness. She was not concerned that she was dying. The breaking of the heart was that her son did not want her. This is something you and I can understand. Mother Teresa.

In this very short but touching story told by Mother Teresa, "Respect" through the conscience has been extremely practicalised.

Respect gotten through the conscience as being the best method to get respect. The conscience is an institution of the mind it gives us the help we need in terms of knowing what's right or wrong in the mind it doesn't affect the physical action of a person, because we can decide not to obey it. Many people know what's right to do because their conscience brings to their minds right things to do but they refuse to oblige.

I define respect through conscience as respect gotten through "love". Where there is love anything is possible and respect is one way we show love. Most broken homes and marriages didn't happen because there was a fight or misunderstanding it happened because there was no more respect.

For love to be real, it must cost, it must hurt, it must empty us of self". Mother Teresa.

For every relationship to grow and last either it be amongst friends, relations, or even in the society, respect is needed. But respect isn't something shown easily, according to Mother Teresa" it must cost, it must hurt, it must empty us of self.

There is this saying.
"if they respect you respect them, if they disrespect you respect them don't reduce your integrity for anyone".
Respect gotten through the

conscience is a state of mind that can't be changed for anyone, because we know it's the right thing to do.

According to Socrates. To know and not to do is really not to know. So if you know how to show respect and don't show it you never knew it.

Knowledge will give power but character respect. Bruce Lee.

So learn to do and not just to know, if you have the knowledge of a thing and you're not known to do it. You're just fooling yourself.

"your joy is determined by doing what you love; while what you love is a clue to your purpose and talents".
Kalensawo.

Respect and Reciprocity.

On his first day in office as president, Abraham Lincoln entered to give his inaugural address, one man stood up. He was a rich Aristocrat. "He said, Mr. Lincoln, you should not forget that your father made shoes for my family" . And the whole senate laughed; they thought they had made of fool of Lincoln.

But certain people are made of a different mettle. Lincoln looked at the man directly in the eye and said, "Sir, I know that my father used to make shoes for your family, and there will be many others here, because he made shoes the way nobody else can.

He was a creator. His shoes were not just shoes; he poured his whole soul into them. I want to ask you, have you any complaint? Because I know how to make shoes myself. If you have any complaint I can make them you another pair of shoes. But as far as I know, nobody has ever complained about my father's shoes. He was a genius, a great creator and am proud of my father.

There's this wide saying that respect is reciprocal, True! respect is but also disrespect. I'm sure the rich aristocrat never forgot that day, he'll wake up every morning remembering how he was embarrassed.

Most people because they are older, richer, or more experienced than their inferior, disrespect them, but they tend to forget the rule of nature that states whatever you sow you'll harvest more in multiple.

Stephen. R. Covey in his book the 7 habits of highly effective people wrote.

"if you want to achieve your highest aspirations and overcome your greatest challenges, identify and apply the principles or natural law that governs the result you seek."

And if the result you seek is to be successful why not try this principle of respect. Among the laws of nature, along with gravity, is the law of karma.

One thing most people do not know is that this very principles also governs every human life.

Pride can be said as trying to go against the law of gravity, many people today want to just become the richest person on earth or the worlds best at which ever aspect they want. But what they forget is the way up is downand the way down is up.

Aeroplanes, jets and even rockets are built for the skies but they weren't built in the skies, to become successful we have to be humble.

Lack of humbleness is one of the greatest factors that brings many great men, nations, and institutions to fall to the ground on their faces. I've seen the airplane many times but it never struck my mind the lessons that can be learnt from it.

I was out for a walk one evening when I noticed an airplane with its headlights shining brightly in the sky, and for the first time, I wondered what the headlights on an airplane were really for; are they just for seeing through the skies or seeing an incoming plane, or are they for something else? Then I realized they weren't really for any of the above; an airplane's headlights are also used to see the runway so that the plane can land safely and avoid crashing.

Many great men when they get to become what they've always dreamt of tend to forget where they came from the runway the runway, forgetting the law of gravity what goes up must come down. They forget to turn on their headlights of respect and humbleness when they are out of strength to keep going and are to come back down will fall with a very loud crash bringing everyone who followed their vision up, down with them.

Thank God for fire fighters most people may survive the crash but the airplane becomes scrap.

Learn from the airplane theory, respect teaches us humbleness which reciprocate support of others. Also when we disrespect others, they'll disrespect us in return.
Respect is just like a magnet which when used properly would pull success.

You can become successful through disrespect but it won't last because it isn't on the right foundation and will one day collapse, but respect does not just get you success it makes it last a lifetime.

How can this problem be solved?

Mary Slessor, a Scottish missionary, became a Christian and taught Bible lessons to children in Nigeria. Despite her alcoholic background, she bravely faced gangs and a ringleader. She saved the lives of slaves, women, and children by learning the local language and battling against the "trial by ordeal" method.

Mary Slessor, a Christian, became a missionary after a woman warned her of the fire of hell. She held Bible classes for children and took groups to the countryside, raising eyebrows among "proper" Christians.

Cutting the long story of Mary

short. In Mary Slessors story we can understand how humanity became her priority because she had gone through pain so she knew what people like her were facing. There's this saying of my mom. "if you can't help others through what used to be your problem you have a problem.

Stephen. R. Covey in his book the 7 habit of highly effective people. Wrote in his foreword about is 19 years old granddaughter. He wrote and I qoute.

Shannon was dragged to serve the people of Romania and wrote Sandra and me an epiphany one day after a little sick child threw up on her and then reached out for a hug. In that moment Shannon resolved "I don't want to live a selfish life anymore". I must spend my life in service."

As of the writing Shannon was back in Romania serving. The way to solve the problem of disrespect is to first have a conscience and a resolve that says," I don't want to live a selfish life anymore". There's this saying everything isn't about you but about everyone.

Mary could have stayed back in Scotland become a drunkard like her father or even worse but she didn't because she didn't want to live a life based on herself. She learnt how to fight her way out of her troubles and taught others also even to get out of worse situations like the killing of twins, cannibalism, and abuse.

She became successful by learning how the problem can be solved, many people today see others struggle in what they've succeeded in but don't even care about them. They say words like.

I didn't put them in the situation, right?

See it's hard to explain, you won't understand.

So what should I do?

How didn't you know this would happen are you a kid?

The problem of respect becoming a scarce commodity can only be solved with virtues like;

*Humility.
*Understanding
*integrity
*trust
*love

You actually can't force people to respect you.... Respect is something that comes as a result of your values and the way you act on them. Tiana.

It's one thing to have the above virtues and another thing to utilize it, according to Tiana respect is something that comes as a result of your values and the way you act on them.

I might know how to love and show respect but if I don't show it, it's just self love.

As a Christian there's this verse of the Bible that always ignite my thoughts is John 3 : 16.

For God so loved the world that He gave is only begotten son that whosoever believe in him should not perish but have everlasting life.

God showed is love to the world by sending His son to save us, so if God being the only solution to the worlds problem of disrespect, can respect the world he created so much to have sent his son to die for us so we do not perish how much more us. According to Mother Teresa love must cost it must hurt it must empty us of self. If God is love and love is Respect. We cannot claim to

Know God and not know respect.

Last words.

In the world which we live respect has become a missing virtue. But that should be in the past now because we can create the change we seek,with what you just learnt in this book and I hope it changes your mindset, behavior and life so that as you begin to work on this things you'll become a better version of you and you'll influence your generation positively.

Share with your family and friends what you have learned and do not forget respect is a key tool to living a successful life as a teenager and as a person we need respect.

OTHER BOOKS BY THE AUTHOR :

* Daily meal planner and grocery list.

* Handwriting workbook for left handed kids.

SOON TO COME:

The Klans successor. A fictional based on an African clan.

This day.

Is love.

Respect a key tool to living a successful life : the leader.